Mem ento Mori

MEMENTO MORI

The Dead
Among Us

PAUL KOUDOUNARIS

THE CHAMPION.

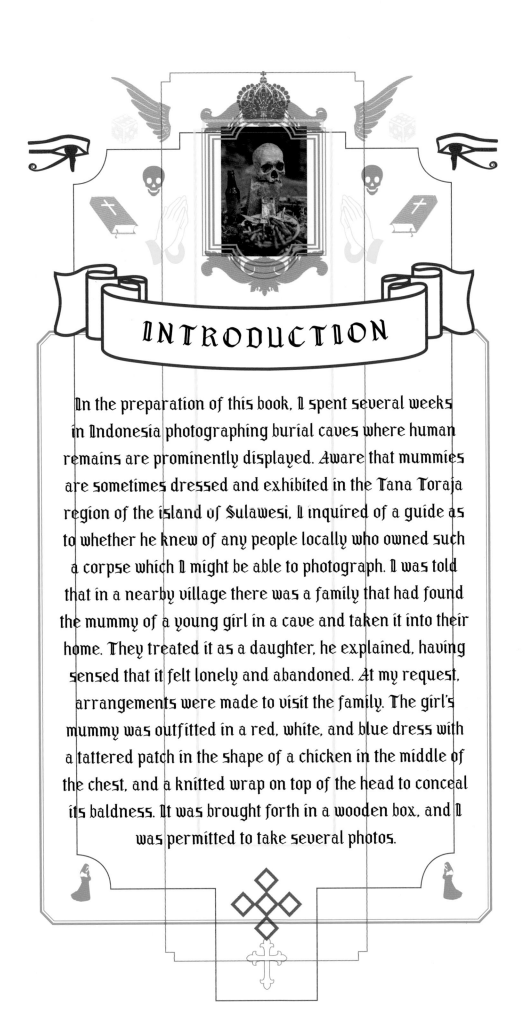

INTRODUCTION

In the preparation of this book, I spent several weeks in Indonesia photographing burial caves where human remains are prominently displayed. Aware that mummies are sometimes dressed and exhibited in the Tana Toraja region of the island of Sulawesi, I inquired of a guide as to whether he knew of any people locally who owned such a corpse which I might be able to photograph. I was told that in a nearby village there was a family that had found the mummy of a young girl in a cave and taken it into their home. They treated it as a daughter, he explained, having sensed that it felt lonely and abandoned. At my request, arrangements were made to visit the family. The girl's mummy was outfitted in a red, white, and blue dress with a tattered patch in the shape of a chicken in the middle of the chest, and a knitted wrap on top of the head to conceal its baldness. It was brought forth in a wooden box, and I was permitted to take several photos.

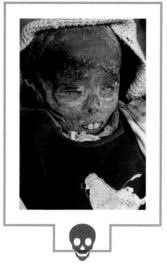

Face of a mummified girl from a small village in the Tana Toraja region of Sulawesi, Indonesia. Discovered in a cave and of unknown provenance, she was taken in as a member of a local household.

Leaving the village, I asked the guide if it was considered unusual to keep mummies in the home. His response was unforgettable. No, he did not find it unusual, because when he was a boy, he and his brothers slept in the same bed as the mummy of their grandfather. He then detailed how each morning the cadaver would be removed from the bed, dressed for the day, and propped up in a corner as if it were standing; later in the evening, it was disrobed and put back to bed. I asked about the motivations for treating his grandfather's mummy as his family had, but felt foolish as I did, because I already knew the answer. Indeed, he turned to me with the nonplussed look one gives people who ask obvious questions. "Because we loved him," he said simply, "and we wanted to preserve for him some part of his daily ritual."

His response was as I had expected. This is not an isolated example of such an intimate and tangible link with the dead, even in the modern world. I had, for instance, spent several years documenting the practice in Bolivia of people keeping in their homes skulls known as *ñatitas* (a nickname meaning "little pug-nosed ones") as companions and helpers, and treating them as esteemed family members. Historically, there have been countless instances of similar relationships to human remains. In the modern Western culture that formed my attitudes, where death unalterably removes a person from the society of the living, that kind of connection is inconceivable. I come from a place where the dead have truly passed on, and the prejudice against them is strong enough that it is hard initially to comprehend the possibility that there may be other ways of relating to them.

18

...slept in the same bed as the mummy of their grandfather.

It can take considerable reflection to understand the extent to which death is not a set term, as we often pretend, but a culturally relative notion. The act of dying can be defined simply as the cessation of life, but what we call death—meaning here a concept that encompasses the questions and anxieties that arise due to the idea of mortality—is a complex intellectual construction. Representing the line of demarcation separating two worlds, it stands before our destiny and occludes it, like a curtain before a stage. As the surrealist writer Georges Bataille noted, death is inherently human.[1] It is only human beings, consciously aware of their own inevitable end, who can contemplate the transition from living state to corpse, and wonder what may lie beyond. Thus, according to Bataille, dying is universal among all creatures, but "death" is ours alone and the way it is approached and understood varies between cultures and historical periods.

Most typically in Western society, death represents a kind of border. Irreversible and impenetrable, it is a boundary beyond which we cannot glimpse or transgress. This attitude is, cross-culturally, in a minority; it has been far more common to consider death as a transition. As Cicero remarked, "That last day does not bring extinction to us, but change of place."[2] When death is conceived of in this way, as a kind of passage or metamorphosis instead of a barrier, an interaction is possible beyond the divide. The dead can still have a role to play as part of a social group, and need not be hidden away and stigmatized. This was certainly the case with the mummies in Tana Toraja. Despite being corpses, both the girl and the grandfather functioned within family units as accepted members of the household.

A woman holds a *ñatita* skull in the chapel of the Cemetery General of La Paz, Bolivia. Such skulls are normally kept in shrines at home and are considered members of the family.

Such stories provide evidence of the kind of bond that has existed between the living and the dead across time and place. From our perspective, of course, to dress corpses and treat them as kin is bizarre to the point of seeming perverse. In Alfred Hitchcock's landmark horror film *Psycho*,[3] it is precisely this act — dressing a cadaver and treating it as a family member — that defines the character of Norman Bates as unequivocally mentally deranged. But such thinking disregards the fact that, despite the modern revulsion to direct encounters with the dead, similar practices were acceptable in Western culture up to fairly modern times. For instance, through the late nineteenth century in parts of Southern Europe, particularly Sicily, it was customary to mummify, dress, display, and visit one's own ancestors. To do so was not a sign of mental illness, but rather, as in Tana Toraja, one of love and respect.

Expressing a connection by displaying the remains of those who have passed on has not only been known in the West, it has been common and even spectacular. History's greatest tableaux in which the living and dead were united into a single social and spiritual fabric are the extravagant ossuaries of pre-Modern Europe, which in sophistication and workmanship trump displays involving death anywhere else in the world. Wherever such sites are found and from whenever they may date, they invariably serve as bridges, creating liminal spaces to unite separated worlds and lost generations. Timeless by nature, they allow the visitor to enter into a quasi-eternity, where life and death, past and present, permanence and dissolution, are all conjoined, and where the intrepid might hope to find some fleeting glimpse of what lies behind the curtain.

19

Such places represent *memento mori* or a "reminder of death"; a term that simply defines an encounter and does not predicate a response or an interpretation. While the modern Western instinct is to find these sites frightening, the people who prepared the remains pictured on the following pages were not doing so to elicit a traumatic reaction. Rather, the creation of *memento mori* has traditionally been intended to serve the greater goal of *memento vitae*, or a "reminder of life." By presenting the specter of death, these spaces affirm life: they ask us to remember those who lived before us, while simultaneously reminding us that our own lives are, and forever will be, linked to theirs in a cycle that is beyond the comprehension of mortal man. This book is a tribute to the profound connection expressed in those sites. It is testimony to the generations of empty sockets and skeletal remains that were once embodied as living flesh, but were then asked to remain among us as witnesses to the universality of the human condition.

String of skulls and crossbones at the Sedlec Ossuary in the Czech Republic. One of the world's most famous macabre sites, the decor was commissioned by a wealthy nobleman who had purchased the old monastic property.

That last day does not bring extinction to us, but change of place.

— CICERO —

Death has been considered a reward as often, if not more so, than it has been considered a punishment. Due to the promise of immortality being a universal staple of theological thought, the act of dying commonly provided a transition to a greater realm. In ancient Persia it was believed that the departed soul would be welcomed into the next world by its own conscience, supplied by a guardian angel with a robe and crown, and reside in the palace of Ahura Mazda. Meanwhile in India, life and death were traditionally understood as parts of a cycle; when that cycle was eventually broken, the result was a return to man's true origins in a realm of pure spirit, the most desirable of all states. The Orphic brotherhoods of Greece thought of the physical body as a prison for the soul, which might after death attain salvation through a reunion with its divine source. This was the view popularized by Plato, who further believed that true knowledge could be acquired only when the soul was liberated from the body, and for this reason a true philosopher has "the desire for death all his life long," forever pursuing it as a means to seek truth.[4]

Woodcut from an *Ars Moriendi* published in Catalonia, Spain, in 1493. Demons lurk in the hope of stealing the soul of a dying man, but by passing on with absolution he is guaranteed salvation.

The Orphic attitude was particularly influential among Early Christians. Birth effectively represented one's actual death since it imprisoned the soul, so the passing of the physical body provided a way to gain entry to eternal life. Mortality was thus not a threat, but a promise of salvation, in which death was, as early luminaries such as St Paul explained, a necessary step, because it freed the soul to reunite with God. Medieval theologians denigrated the living corpus as reprehensible—St Bernard, for instance, called it "nothing but stinking sperm, a sack of excrement and food for worms."[5] The physical body was corrupt, and for centuries death was considered by both the pious and the intellectual as a treasured release. St Teresa of Avila was joyous on her deathbed, exclaiming, "How I have longed for thee! O welcome hour—the end of exile!"[6] René Descartes, meanwhile, greeted passing with the words, "My soul, you have been held captive a long time. This is the time for you to leave prison and relinquish the burden of this body."[7]

20

This enthusiasm is characteristic of what the French scholar of mortality Philippe Ariès termed the "tame death." It was a concept that found beauty in accepting one's own end, and Ariès argued that it held sway for at least two millennia, if not all the way back to prehistoric times.[8] In the medieval Christian world on which he based the bulk of his study, a proper death was an important rite of passage. Exiting one's body was a deliberate process that started with understanding the imminence of death and making preparations to meet it. All worldly issues would be resolved beforehand, and for the actual passing, a retinue of loved ones and friends would be gathered, turning it into a community rather than private affair. A highly ritualized act, dying well required the participation of a priest to administer Absolution, Confession, Communion, and Extreme Unction, and the lighting of candles and incense to create a proper aesthetic environment.

Demons again lurk at the moment of passing in a fifteenth-century German *Ars Moriendi*, but the man's soul, depicted as a small, naked person, has been delivered into the hands of an angel.

Death was such a prominent topic that by the start of the fourteenth century an entire genre of literature had emerged that would continue to be popular for the next 300 years: *Ars Moriendi*, or "The Art of Dying," to guide people to the best and most productive means of exiting the mortal coil. Authors on the process of confronting death explained that passing on was "the breaking of all bonds of this cursed and evil world...and entry into joy and glory."[9] People were urged to understand that "death unto the good man is the end of all evils," and told to "cast out the world and learn to die."[10] Dying should not start on the deathbed, however, but rather be the culmination of a lifetime spent contemplating and accepting one's mortality. As the seventeenth-century English theologian Jeremy Taylor said in a renowned book on *Holy Dying*, "He that would die well must always look for death, every day knocking at the gates of the grave."[11] Or, as the famed Italian Renaissance preacher Girolamo Savonarola put it, "If you want to do well and escape from sin, have a strong fantasy of death." He urged his followers to acclimatize themselves to passing on by visiting the dying and attending funerals. "These are the eyeglasses that I am talking about," he continued, "keep death always impressed in your fantasy, and in every work of yours, remember death."[12]

How I have longed for thee! O welcome hour – the end of exile!

—
ST TERESA
OF AVILA

Savonarola's exhortation was a longstanding refrain. As a symbol, the *memento mori* is universal—for example, it was an encounter with a corpse that awakened in the Buddha his concern for the suffering of mankind, and the desire to find a means to remedy it.[13] In the West, confronting death was considered an all-purpose palliative, effective in suppressing vanity, and instilling important lessons about the temporal nature of the human body. Death was not only a staple in the repertoires of visual artists, it was also part of the general tableau of life. Confraternities dedicated to the dead were found in many European communities, and their macabre sentiments were often publicly displayed. The artists' biographer Giorgio Vasari related an account of a "horrible and surprising" train of death designed by the painter Piero di Cosimo for such a brotherhood in Florence. Pulled by buffalo and painted with skulls and crossbones, the top of the large car featured a grim reaper wielding a scythe, and graves that opened to reveal figures dressed as skeletons.[14] One of the most famous of these brotherhoods, the Confraternita dell'Orazione e Morte in Rome, would for religious holidays produce spectacular public exhibitions based around themes of mortality—for example, creating displays of Purgatory from mountains of human bones engulfed in flames.[15]

The most prominent displays of death, however, were in the charnel houses of church cemeteries and crypts. Great quantities of bones were kept in these spaces, allowing a face-to-face encounter with the past. The word "charnel" derived from the Latin *caro*, meaning flesh, and referred to a place to store human remains. Its synonym "ossuary" came from *os*, meaning bone, and originally referred to a box used to hold individual remains, later expanded as an architectural term. There was nothing unique about the construction of such sites by Christians. As the plates of this book show, the conservation and display of human remains as a means to venerate the dead is cross-culturally common. It dates back to at least the Neolithic Middle East and Europe, when the skull received particular attention; caches of exhumed crania dating as far back as 8,500 BC have been found. These were frequently coated with layers of plaster or bitumen, with facial details added in paint, shells, or other materials, and apparently displayed as totems to allow the living access to the life forces of those who had passed on.[16]

IL RIPOSO ETERNO
DÁ LORO O SIGNORE
E LA LVCE PERPETVA
RISPLENDA LORO
RIPOSINO IN PACE

21

It was among Early Christians, however, that the fetishization of human bones most flourished. Adherents to the new faith believed that the resurrected body would be a continuation of the earthly corpus and therefore chose to preserve it through burial, preferably in churchyards where the deceased would be under the protection of the saints to whom the sanctuary was dedicated. Since churchyards tended to be small spaces, old remains were commonly removed to free room for the newly deceased, but the exhumed bones still needed to be preserved on consecrated ground. The most effective solution for storage was the charnel house, where the disinterred remains could be safe while they waited to be reanimated and clothed in Divine Glory. These structures were popularized in Middle Eastern monastic cemeteries, which traditionally had room for only a handful of burials, making the spatial constraints particularly acute. It may never be possible to determine the very first Christian charnel house, but they are recorded in existence by the sixth century, and the trend eventually migrated to Western Europe. It caught on especially in Austria, Bavaria, the Upper Rhine, and parts of Italy and France, and by the thirteenth century charnels were practically ubiquitous.

Entrance to the crypt of the Confraternita dell'Orazione e Morte, Rome, where passages once led to the brotherhood's catacombs. Now destroyed, these held thousands of skeletal remains, which were used in public spectacles on the topic of mortality.

By the medieval period in Europe, charnel houses such as this one in Mistail, Switzerland, had become popular not just as storage spaces for bones, but as places to contemplate mortality.

Over time, it became typical to use the bones to create displays within the charnels. Remains would be stacked into walls of often impressive height, and the rooms were provided with windows or grates, so passersby could see the contents. Such spaces reminded the living of the need to redeem themselves, and their displays were powerful enough that moralists considered them the best possible bulwark against worldly pride. People were instructed to visit these places, in passages that urged them to "descend into the Vault or Charnel-house, and by serious consideration how short their Time is, to inforce upon themselves a care of redeeming it."[17] Traditional slogans were often presented among the bones, to further emphasize the transience of human life and the connection between the living and the dead. Several are preserved. In Naters, Switzerland, for example, a sign above the bone stack in the ossuary reads, *Was ihr seid, das waren wir/Was wir sind/das wirdet ihr* ("What you will be is what we are. What we are is what you will be"), and the entrance to the large charnel house in Evora, Portugal, is inscribed over the doorway with the words, *Nos ossos que aqui estamos pelos vossos esparamos* ("We bones that are here await yours"). Sometimes mottos would be painted directly on the bones themselves, especially skulls, where they would be placed on the forehead. This trend was most common in Bavaria and the Alps, and began at some sites as early as the fifteenth century. Recorded examples include: "Who was the idiot and who was the sage, who was the beggar and who was the emperor?"; "We the dead lie here in the charnel and no one with you is more powerful than we"; as well as *vanitas* phrases such as "Was I beautiful or ugly?"; "Was I loved or not?"; and "Was I rich or poor?."[18]

The charnel houses were more than just immersive *memento mori*, however. An important part of the ritual landscape of the Christian world, they often included an altar or conjoined chapel, to be used in services honoring the dead. Commonly referred to by terms such as "soul chambers,"[19] the bone rooms allowed visitors to reach across the mysterious gap and interact with the deceased. They were places where prayers could be offered to lessen the suffering of those who were now in Purgatory, and, in return for this charity, those who had passed on were expected to intercede in worldly concerns. Thus, in places such as the Fontanelle Cemetery in Naples—a giant cave ossuary that was among the most famous sites where the living would commune with the dead—people would adopt skulls, enshrine and provide prayers for them, and then ask the souls to help them in domestic matters, health issues, and affairs of the heart.

Untold examples of this kind of exchange survive from across Europe over several centuries, and the dead were thought to share the concerns of the living even in mundane details. In the charnel in Maria Worth, Austria, for instance, skulls were found with the numbers one to ninety inscribed on them—these were the numbers of the local lottery, and apparently the souls were being asked to predict the winning combinations. Exactly how they were expected to communicate the numbers to the living in Maria Worth was not recorded, but attempts to divine lottery combinations using the bones in ossuaries were also reported in Italy, Germany, and the Czech Republic.[20] A story is recorded of a weaver in the Upper Palatinate who removed a skull from a charnel and placed it under his pillow in the hope that it would channel the lucky numbers to him in a dream.

What you will be is what we are. What we are is what you will be.

The deceased did indeed offer a message: apparently unconcerned with such a petty issue, he demanded that his skull be returned.[21] This was not the only soul with something to say, and many traditions involved literal dialogues with the dead. In parts of Brittany, it was believed that on holidays skulls were able to speak, especially in the port town of Treguier, where it was claimed that on Halloween they would describe their circumstances in the other world, even naming those who would die during the next year.[22]

Yet the most poignant message the bones would communicate was a symbolic one, involving the connection between generations. The removal of osteological material from cemetery to ossuary was usually performed in the presence of the closest surviving relatives, with children born since the person had passed being encouraged to directly handle the remains of their ancestor. Especially when the bones were inscribed with the identities of the deceased, they provided a means to help establish family bonds. It is recorded that in Hallstatt, Austria, where the charnel is famous for possessing the largest surviving cache of painted skulls (over 600 are preserved), adults would use the display to introduce children to their own lineage. Pointing out the crania of long-passed relatives, they would recount stories about the people in question, with the skulls creating a kind of snapshot of family history.[23] This practice is documented through the mid-nineteenth century, but by this date it was considered a hopeless provincial anachronism. The reign of death was nearing an end—in Europe, the bonds between the living and the dead would soon be dissolved.

Painted skulls such as these in Hallstatt, Austria, were part of a long tradition of recording the name of the deceased directly on the bones; the practice was also popular in Germany and Switzerland.

23

Many charnel houses with impressive displays still exist, such as this one in Naters, Switzerland, but they have ceased to be important spiritual sites and are now seen as historical curiosities.

Death is depicted as a victor in the frontispiece to the 1682 book *Theatrum mortis humanae tripartium*. By the twentieth century, death had become the Western world's most ruthless adversary.

The concept of a "denial of death" can be dated to a 1915 essay by Sigmund Freud, in which the pioneering psychoanalyst studied contemporary attitudes towards mortality in relation to World War I. Modern man wants to "put death on one side, to eliminate it from life. We tried to hush it up," he concluded.[24] Freud would be seconded two decades later by the German philosopher and essayist Walter Benjamin. "Dying was once a public process in the life of the individual and a most exemplary one," he wrote, ". . . (but) in the course of modern times dying has been pushed further out of the perceptual world of the living."[25]

What Freud and Benjamin were identifying was a change in the relationship to death in Western culture that by the early twentieth century had become obvious, but the seeds of which can be found as far back as the Reformation. Even during the glory days of the sixteenth and seventeenth centuries, when the display of the dead in Europe was at its most ostentatious, there was a growing clamor to put the dead to rest. Protestants considered the popular rites surrounding the mounds of bones in the charnel houses to be superstitious vestiges of Catholicism that needed to be rooted out in areas that had left the Church. With few exceptions, old bone houses were dismantled in these areas in order to discourage members of the community who might be attracted to them as places of power, magic, or healing.[26]

24

> ...it outdoes all other accidents because it is the last of them.
>
> — R.L. STEVENSON —

Protestants were especially repulsed by the idea that the dead might be placed within a sanctuary, which they considered to be a form of defilement. "Through the false Conceit of Charity to the Dead, (Christians) have forgot, the veneration due to God's House, & turned churches into Charnel Houses," fulminated the eighteenth-century scholar and Anglican reverend Thomas Lewis.[27] The opinions expressed by Early Modern critics are close enough to current attitudes that it is easy to see in them the birth of our present-day relationship with the dead. "The burial of the dead is done for the living, not the dead, since they have no sense of how they are deposited," Lewis continued, and he further argued that the presence of the dead should be avoided as a potential hygiene risk.[28]

Extravagant displays of mortality, such as this one at Santa Maria della Concezione in Rome, once had theological importance in the Catholic Church but were later looked upon as strange or suspicious.

Such critiques of the traditional cult of the dead were in the short term not only ineffectual in curbing such practices, they actually inspired the Catholics to create even greater displays of human remains than any that had come before. On the side of the Church, it was standard Counter Reformation ideology to emphasize as virtuous and inherently Catholic anything the Reformers rejected and despised. When it came to displaying the dead, this was especially the case with monastic orders such as the Capuchins, for whom morbid aesthetics seemed to function as a badge of honor and guarantor against worldly pride. The result was a kind of golden age of art in human bone. Many of the surviving Counter Reformation macabre sites stand as masterpieces of art celebrating death. These include the spectacular ossuary in the crypt of the monastery of Santa Maria della Concezione in Rome, as well as several elaborate funerary chapels and catacomb systems lined with mummies in Southern Italy and Sicily. Equally impressive spaces would continue to be built in Catholic areas for the next three centuries.

Over time, and especially during the Enlightenment, many Catholics would start to feel the same way as their Protestant detractors about such displays. The idea that the dead were a pollutant—both hygienically and symbolically—gained currency, and during the late eighteenth century, especially in France, churchyard cemeteries were emptied and charnel houses closed down, even by Catholics. Removed from public view, during the nineteenth century the dead were shifted away from urban centers to a new type of site: cemeteries that were non-denominational rather than being affiliated with a specific church or parish, spread over large tracts of land in the suburbs. These provided a model that would eventually spawn the modern funerary industry. Michel Foucault, one of the pre-eminent philosophers of the second half of the twentieth century, called the traditional abodes of the dead "the sacred and immortal heart of the city," but they were now exiled to newly constructed ghettoes.[29]

Cemeteries such as Père Lachaise in Paris are of great beauty, but they were part of the first wave of large, suburban burial grounds that formed the basis of the modern funeral industry.

There were other factors coalescing to oust the dead, including a new conception of the body, in which public versus private boundaries were redefined. The Russian literary critic Mikhail Bakhtin considered the medieval idea of corporeality to be based on a "grotesque body," with less differentiated limits than those of modern, polite society. Acts of "bodily drama"—including birth, defecation, copulation, and ultimately death—were at one time played out on a public stage. In contrast, the impression that had taken hold by the nineteenth century was of a *homo clausus*, a closed body, privatized from the world, and protected as the domain of the individual.[30] To look beyond that boundary was uncouth, and displays of human remains now seemed voyeuristic and crude.

25

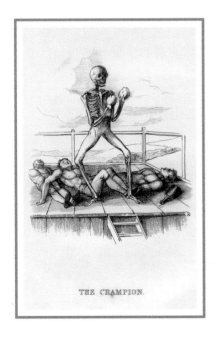

Image from the painter and poet Richard Dagley's 1827 *Death's Doings*, a book that explained how death intervenes in people's lives. In the end, death is left standing, unconquerable.

The twentieth-century philosopher Jean Baudrillard believed that the Western separation from death was inevitable. As anchors to the past in a society that preferred to look to the future, the dead created anxiety. In the complex web of our progress, Baudrillard theorized, they signified decomposition not just of the individual, but of culture as a whole, and it was necessary to cast them off as a form of emancipation.[31] By the nineteenth century, the "tame death" that Ariès had noted was giving way to a drastically new version, one which the early American psychologist William James called "the worm at the core" of our pretensions to happiness.[32] Death became something shattering, menacing, and fearful. One of the first to give full expression to this new force was Robert Louis Stevenson. The famed author wrote an 1878 essay on the subject, seeing in death not a release and passage, but a dreadful foe that leaves in its wake "a mocking, tragical, and soon intolerable residue" of emptiness. "The changes wrought by death are in themselves so sharp and final, so terrible and melancholy in their consequences," he continued, "that the thing stands alone in man's experience, and has no parallel . . . it outdoes all other accidents because it is the last of them."[33]

In this fifteenth-century block book about the Antichrist, death is perceived as threatening damnation. By the mid-twentieth century, the threat was no longer spiritual but rather one which brought dissolution of being.

It is interesting to note that Stevenson terms death an "accident," as if it were an unfortunate slip, rather than an inevitable process. This attitude became characteristically modern, as advancements in medical science further altered our perception of death. The act of dying had once been familiar, with people passing away at home surrounded by friends and relatives. Now typically occurring in hospitals, however, death has become a clinical phenomenon devoid of traces of intimacy. Measured and qualified by physicians, it has even been broken into different categories: brain death, biological death, and cellular death. In this antiseptic atmosphere, rather than being natural and necessary, the act of dying constitutes a model failure — a failure of the individual body to continue, and a failure of the physician to achieve a cure. The "tame death" of medieval Europe had been a public and beautiful act; modern death on the other hand is ugly, and Foucault called it "the most private and shameful thing of all."[34]

A further nail in the coffin was the increasing secularization of the modern world. Bataille believed that the stigma surrounding death is based on feelings of impotence in relation to the subject, since it marks the limit of what we can conceive and forces questions about cosmic realities we cannot answer.[35] Of course, religion traditionally provided an antidote to such feelings by promising immortality. Mitigating death is perhaps the most important function of a religion, and the "tame death" that Ariès wrote about was in truth made docile by the unquestioned belief that beyond the divide was the glory of Heaven. As religion lost its hold in the West, death went from being the soul's release from prison to being a prison in its own right, one that threatened total loss of being. Ironically, various psychological studies indicate that displays of mortality may be beneficial and comforting, since such encounters not only help people overcome fears of their own passing, but in general also contribute to greater vivacity.[36] Perhaps, on reflection, the modern world needs *memento mori* more than ever, but the *timor mortis* (fear of death) that has become rampant along with increasing secularization has ensured that visible reminders of death are removed from daily life.

26

Even into the early twentieth century, death continued to be intimate and familiar in some areas. These post-mortem photos show families at home with their deceased in Estonia (top) and Bulgaria (bottom).

By the mid-twentieth century, Western psychoanalysis had begun to look on the absolute fear of death as something innate to the human condition. It was considered the very basis of our instinct for self-preservation. A fear of such magnitude could be paralyzing to the individual, the theories held, but fortunately it tended to be repressed. It was nevertheless believed to be ever-present in man's mental functioning.[37] The subject became a cultural taboo, and in an essay from 1955 the anthropologist Geoffrey Gorer likened death to a kind of pornography, rejected by polite society as disgusting and prurient, and with which any obsession should be discouraged.[38] This version of death provided outstanding antagonists for horror film audiences — after all, it was considered everyone's innate and primal fear — but would render the dead inappropriate partners for the living. The act of dying was surrounded with such negativity that the sociologist David Moller recalled a curious exchange in the introduction to his book *Confronting Death: Values, Institutions, and Human Mortality*. In preparing the book, he had contacted the American Cancer Society and requested permission to include some of their materials. But they refused to allow it, responding, "Absolutely not. In no way do we want to be associated with a book on death. We want to emphasize the positive aspects of cancer only."[39] Death had been rejected as an unworthy partner even for cancer.

Direct encounters with the dead are now rare in Western culture, occurring primarily at wakes or funerals. Even then, mortality is not truly acknowledged, but rather hidden in closed boxes, or camouflaged under heavy layers of make-up. The situation was once very different, and death was welcomed at rites of passing. It is recorded that at a 1572 funeral service for Sigismund II Augustus, King of Poland and Grand Duke of Lithuania, the church was completely decorated with skeletons holding scythes.[40] Meanwhile, the 1574 memorial for Duke Cosimo de' Medici also involved skeletons, holding banderoles with slogans about mortality.[41] There was even a popular practice during the Baroque period in Italy of placing a mannequin in the deceased's armor and have it ride into the church on a horse during the funeral service. When this phantom eventually fell to the floor with a noisy clattering, it was understood as an emphatic and poignant symbol of passing.

Capable of housing thousands of bodies, this cold storage room at the Los Angeles County Coroner's office is typical of the modern face of death, with intimacy and bonding replaced by clinical detachment.

This kind of gesture—in effect, inviting death to a funeral—would nowadays be considered in bad taste, perhaps as an inappropriate joke. To modern sensibilities, the palatable and decorous alternative is having funeral parlor staff attempt to recreate the corpse as a simulacrum of its former self. As anyone who has attended the viewings of corpses can attest, the results of the morticians' labors, no doubt well-intentioned, can sometimes be painfully amiss. But apparently anything is better than confronting death on its own terms. Baudrillard cannily remarked that "death exists only when society discriminates against the dead."[42] So it is that in Western culture, the dead have truly passed on. But as the following pages show, they once peacefully coexisted with the living, and continue to in many areas of the world.

(1) Georges Bataille, *Death and Sensuality: A Study of Exorcism and the Taboo* (New York: 1977). (2) Cicero, *M. Tullii Ciceronis Tusculanarum disputationum libbi [sic] V. Cum commentario Joannis Davisii,…Editio quarta. Huic editioni accedunt Richardi Bentleii emendationes, cum indice rerum & verborum* (London: 1738), I, 49. (3) The film is based on Robert Bloch's 1959 book of the same title, although the film has become considerably more familiar. (4) The comment is made in Plato's *Phaedo*, 64a. (5) From St Bernard's *Meditations*, quoted in Piero Camporesi, *The Incorruptible Flesh: Bodily Mutation and Mortification in Religion and Folklore*, trans. Tania Croft-Murray (Cambridge: 1988), 77–78. (6) Quoted in Virginia Moore, *Ho for Heaven! Man's Changing Attitude Toward Dying* (New York: 1946), 149. (7) Desmond M. Clark, *Descartes: A Biography* (Cambridge: 2006), 408. (8) Philippe Ariès, *The Hour of Our Death*, trans. Helen Weaver (New York: 1981), 5–92. (9) The quote is from a French translation of the *Speculum artis moriendi*, c.1490. Quoted in *The Art and Craft to Know Well to Die*, an abridgement of *The Book of the Craft of Dying*, translated from the French by W. Caxton, in *The book of the Craft of Dying, and other early English tracts concerning death*, ed. Francis M.M. Comper, intro. Rev. George Congreve (London: 1917), 57. (10) Ibid., 130. (11) Jeremy Taylor, *Rule and Exercises of Holy Dying*, ed. P.G. Stanwood (Oxford: 1989), 49. The book was originally published in 1651. (12) Quoted in Pierroberto Scarmella, "The Italy of Triumphs and Contrasts," in *Human Fragilitas: The Themes of Death in Europe from the Thirteenth Century to the Eighteenth Century*, ed. Alberto Tenenti (Clusone: 2002) 25–98, 58. The quote is from a sermon given by Savonarola in 1496, which was transcribed by a follower and published under the title *Predica dell'arte del ben morire*. (13) The encounter is one of the "four sights" that would change the Buddha while he was still a young prince by the name of Gautama. The first was an old man, followed by a sick man, and then the corpse itself, which made an indelible impression on him. The fourth sight was a holy man, and this inspired in him the desire to follow that example and seek an end to suffering. (14) Giorgio Vasari, *The Lives of the Painters, Sculptors, and Architects*, vol. 2, ed. and intro. William Gaunt (New York: 1963), 177–178. (15) Susan Vandiver Nicassio, *Imperial City: Rome, Romans, and Napoleon, 1796–1815* (Garden City, UK: 2005), 115, 126. (16) There are several sources on this topic, but see in particular "Complexity in Context: Plain, Painted, and Modeled Skulls from the Neolithic Middle East," in *Skull Collection, Modification and Decoration*, ed. Michelle Bonogofsky (Oxford: 2006) 15–28. (17) *The gentleman's calling, written by the Author of the Whole Duty of Man* (London: 1677), 105. (18) Marie Andree-Eysn, *Volkskundliches: Aus dem Bayrisch-Österreichischen Alpengebiete* (Braunschweig: 1910), 155. (19) *Seelenkapelle*, for example, was a common name in some German-speaking regions. (20) Andree-Eysn, 150–151. (21) Ibid., 151. (22) Ibid., 152. (23) Torstein Svojold mentions this use of the skulls in his essay "Testing Assumptions for Skeletal Studies by Means of Identified Skulls from Hallstatt, Austria," in *Grave Reflections: Portraying the Past Through Cemetery Studies*, eds. Shelly Rae Saunders and Ann Herring (Toronto: 1995), 241–281. (24) The essay was included in the 1915 "Thoughts for the Times on War and Death." See *The Pelican Freud Library*, vol. 12 (Harmondsworth: 1985), 77–78. (25) Benjamin's original essay was written in 1936. See Walter Benjamin, *Illuminations*, ed. and intro. Hannah Arendt, trans. Harry Zohn (New York: 1969), 93–94. (26) There are many sources for the topics noted in this paragraph. In particular, see Craig Koslofsky, *The Reformation of the Dead: Death and Ritual in Early Modern Germany, 1450–1700* (New York: 2000) and Paul Koudounaris, *The Empire of Death: A Cultural History of Ossuaries and Charnel Houses* (London: 2011), 64–65. (27) Thomas Lewis, *Churches no Charnel Houses* (London: 1726), 5. (28) Ibid. (29) Michel Foucault, "Of Other Spaces: Utopias and Heterotopias," trans. Jay Miskowiec (originally published as "Des Espace Autres" in *Architecture/Mouvement/Continuité*, March 1967), accessed at: http://web.mit.edu/allanmc/www/foucault1.pdf; 6. (30) See Mikhail Bakhtin, *Rabelais and his World*, trans. Hélène Iswolsky (Bloomington: 1984), 303–367, and Norbert Elias, *The Civilizing Process: Sociogenetic and Psychogenetic Investigations*, trans. Edmund Jephcott (Oxford: 2000; rev. edn.), 472. (31) Jean Baudrillard, *Symbolic Exchange and Death*, trans. Iain Hamilton Grant (London: 1995). (32) William James, *Varieties of Religious Experience: A Study in Human Nature* (New York: 1958), 121. The essay was originally published in 1902. (33) Robert Louis Stevenson, *Aes Triplex* (Westport, CN: 1944; reprint edition), 1–4. (34) The quote comes from a lecture Foucault gave while conducting research on power and sexuality. See Benjamin Noys, *The Culture of Death* (Oxford: 2005), 32. (35) Bataille, 140–141. (36) The studies are cited in Christopher Alexander *et al. A Pattern Language: Towns, Buildings, Construction* (New York: 1977), 354. In this book on city planning the authors advise that memorials involving mortality be prominently placed within cities. (37) This psychology of death is best summarized in Ernest Becker's book *The Denial of Death* (New York: 1973). (38) Geoffrey Gorer, "The Pornography of Death," *Encounter 25*, October 1955 (49–52). (39) David Moller, *Confronting Death: Values, Institutions, and Human Mortality* (New York: 1996), vii. (40) Scarmella, 64. (41) Ibid. (42) Baudrillard, 144.

The Dead Will Rise

MACABRE MASTERPIECES OF THE NINETEENTH CENTURY

💀　💀　💀

When Frantisek Rint left his signature in bones on the wall of the Sedlec Ossuary in the Czech Republic (opposite), he was placing his mark on an artistic triumph. Hired to create elaborate designs in an old monastic charnel house, his labors resulted in the most famous monument ever decorated in human remains. Rint was only one of countless craftsmen to have worked in human bone, a medium that reached its zenith in the nineteenth century, when another great masterpiece, the Paris Catacombs, was also constructed. By the time these monuments were completed, the West's relationship to the dead had already begun to change, and Sedlec and Paris were left as the last and most extravagant relics of a glorious past.

The ossuary in Sedlec (pp.28–41) was built in a small chapel on the property of a Cistercian monastery. One of the abbots took a pilgrimage to the Holy Land and returned with a handful of dirt said to be from Golgotha, which was used to consecrate a cemetery. People from throughout Europe made arrangements to be buried in this hallowed ground, and the demand for space combined with periodic outbreaks of epidemics to ensure that it was consistently full. Older burials had to be exhumed to create room for new ones, with the remains stored in the chapel. During the seventeenth century, the bones were arranged in a series of large pyramids topped with crowns, to symbolize the Kingdom of God, and the building became a popular place for people to contemplate their own mortality.

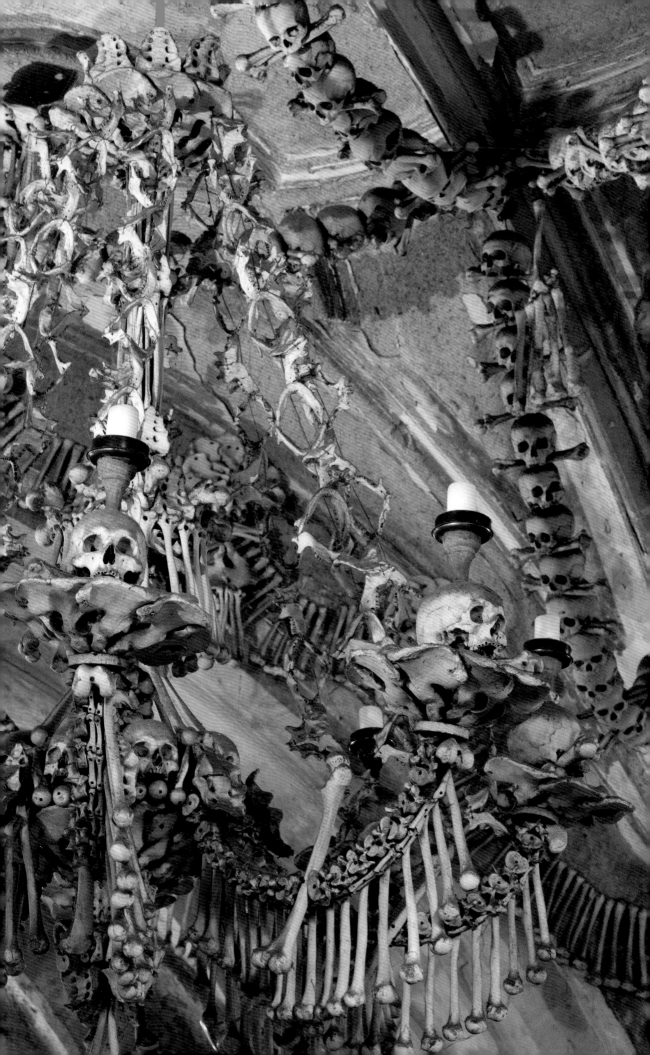

Rint's reconstruction of the ossuary was funded by Karl Joseph Adolph von Schwarzenberg, a member of a longstanding noble line. The monastery had been secularized and the property acquired by his family in the early nineteenth century, and it was decided in the 1860s to update the chapel and create a macabre showpiece with the bones. Among the devices the artist fashioned were spires and garlands made from skulls and crossbones, and replicas of ecclesiastic items such as monstrances and chalices. Two signature pieces of incredible intricacy and delicacy assure the ossuary's fame: an eight-foot-diameter chandelier said to contain one of every bone in the human body (p.34; opposite), and a replica of the Schwarzenberg family coat of arms (above).

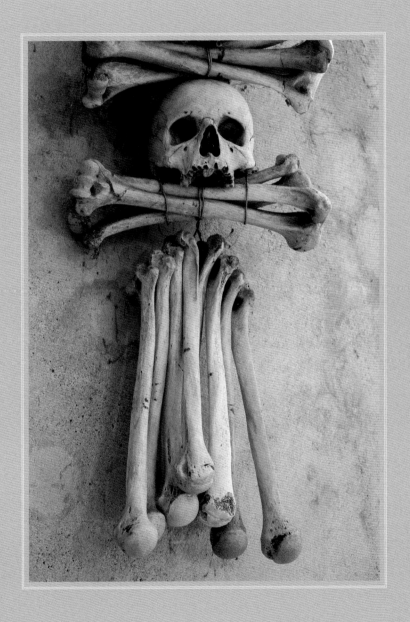

Work had begun on the century's other great monument in bone, the Paris Catacombs (below; opposite), sixty years before Rint began his reconstructions at Sedlec. The passageways themselves were centuries older: they were tunnels that had been left behind when rock was quarried for construction in the city's center. Eighteenth-century debates about the hygiene of overflowing graveyards resulted in a decree that Paris's urban cemeteries be evacuated—it was decided that the remains could be placed in the old passageways, and in 1786, the solemn transfer of millions of dead began. In 1810 the Emperor Napoleon approved a plan by Louis-Étienne Héricart de Thury, the Inspector-General of Quarries, to arrange the bones in decorative patterns and open the newly rechristened "Catacombs" to the public as the world's greatest *memento mori*.

Construction in the Catacombs continued until nearly the end of the nineteenth century, following a basic design devised by Thury, with femurs and fibulae stacked to knee level, then a line of skulls that was topped by more long bones, and finally capped with another row of skulls. Among the bones were also placed religious symbols, placards containing *memento mori* slogans, and carved stones indicating from which cemeteries the bones had been exhumed. Special memorials were also created, including a sepulchral lamp, pillars of remembrance, and at the very end of the pedestrian route through the Catacombs, *La Rotonde des Tibias* (above), a thick cylinder of thousands of tibiae. When Thury's dream finally became reality, it stood as far and away the world's largest ossuary, spanning some 11,000 square meters.

The Gates of Paradise

BONES AND SALVATION IN THE CHRISTIAN TRADITION

💀 💀 💀

The elaborate constructions at Paris and Sedlec evolved from humble bone rooms that had initially been popular in Middle Eastern monasteries. Such properties had limited numbers of graves, so it was necessary to exhume previous burials to make room for the newly deceased. To preserve the bones on consecrated ground, charnels were constructed adjacent to the cemetery. The oldest extant example is found at St Catherine's Monastery in Sinai, Egypt (opposite; p.47). Built in the sixth century, it is composed of two sections: one for skulls, the other for miscellaneous body parts. Such bone rooms eventually became popular in Greece and are still in use on Mount Athos, where monasteries maintain traditionally small cemeteries, requiring the monks to continually exhume and store remains (p.47).

45

The need to find a place to store disinterred remains was also a concern in Western Europe, where charnels started to become popular during the medieval period. They were constructed from Italy in the south to England in the north, and in some areas churches were mandated to build them. Most of the early bone rooms in the West were little more than storage areas, where remains were piled in a disorganized way. The small ossuary at Roncesvalles, Spain (below), which dates to Carolingian times, is an example of what an early medieval charnel may have looked like. Others, such as the ossuary in Wamba, Spain (pp.50–51), retain a similarly humble appearance: individually, the skulls are dramatic, but the arrangement of the bones is simple.

Over time, churches started creating more orderly displays in their charnels. With the bones stacked high against the walls and prominence given to skulls, these spaces became more compelling exhibits of *memento mori*. The charnels were opened to public view and people were urged to look upon them and contemplate the inevitability of death. Traditional religious symbolism also began to be added; motifs from the Crucifixion being particularly popular. At the Swiss ossuaries in Stans (below), Naters (p.54), and Leuk (p.55), sculptures of this kind are still found in front of the bones. The overwhelming theme of the charnels was of course mortality, but by adding the Crucifixion to the display, visitors were reminded that through Christ's sacrifice even death could be overcome.

Especially in Germany, Austria, and Switzerland, it was common to find bone rooms built next to funerary chapels. Known as *Karnerkappelen* (charnel chapels), the sanctuaries themselves did not actually contain bones, but were instead used to honor the recently deceased and for services on holidays connected to death and resurrection. The largest surviving German ossuary, at Oppenheim, was attached to such a funerary chapel. Visitors would enter the bone room to commune with the dead, and many of the skulls show a worn patch on the forehead (below), the result of people rubbing them in the belief that they possessed supernatural power. However, the most curious feature at Oppenheim—a golden skull set into the wall (opposite)—is not original it was painted by a movie production company that filmed in the ossuary

In Africa, Christian ossuaries were
sporadically found all the way down to
Ethiopia, where the magnificent cave church
of Yemrehanna Kristos still maintains a
sprawling charnel ground (pp.58–63).
Constructed in the eleventh century in
alternating layers of wood and stone, the
church was built by a king of the same name,
noted for his piety and considered a saint.
The belief that Yemrehanna Kristos himself
was buried in the cave caused it to become
an important pilgrimage site. Many visitors
would die either along the arduous route or
at the church, and their remains accumulated
in the back of the cave, eventually covering the
ground with a thick layer of broken coffins,
brittle bones, and withered funerary shrouds.

Set high atop Mount Abuna Josef, Yemrehanna Kristos remained isolated
from the outside world for nearly a millennium. For the estimated 5,000
people who made the trek and found lasting peace there, to be laid to rest
at Yemrehanna Kristos was to die in a blessed state. The cave continues to
draw pilgrims, and hermits and priests still live nearby. Meanwhile, the
bone yard is preserved as a reminder of all those pious visitors who made
this sacred spot their final destination. No matter their location, all of the
early Christian charnels were united in the belief that the bones of those
who had passed were a potent symbol for the living. Yet the Christians
were not the only ones preserving human bones.

They Walk Among Us

💀   💀   💀

The desire to display the remains
of those who have passed on is not
unique to the Christian world. In some
areas of Asia, bones would be used to
decorate caves, with the most famous
examples found in Indonesia, in the
Tana Toraja region of the island of
Sulawesi. In Torajan culture, it was
common for villages to use nearby caves
as cemeteries. The deceased were placed
in wooden coffins, which would inevitably
deteriorate in the humid tropical climate,
and the bones were then arranged for
public viewing. Burial caves were not
considered to be places of death, because
the spirits of the dead lived on within
them. Wooden effigies known as "tau tau"
(opposite; p.68) were often carved and
placed within the display as a reminder
of that spiritual presence.

65

Death in Torajan culture represents a transition of unparalleled importance: it is not believed to be a sudden occurrence, but rather a stage in a gradual process that eventually leads to *Puya*, or the land of souls. The funerals that commemorate this passage are the most elaborate events in Torajan society, so expensive that it may take years for the family of the deceased to raise enough money. Services honoring high-ranking people can attract thousands of guests and last for up to a week, with the deceased wrapped in layers of cloth and serenaded by singing, chanting, and flute music. The effort and expense are necessary to ensure the dead pass to the afterlife, because until the funeral is completed the dead are believed to continue lingering around the village.

After the funeral ceremonies, the deceased is placed in a coffin and taken
to a burial cave. The coffins are often placed on slats of wood or suspended
with ropes—the higher one's social status, the more elevated one's coffin.
Inevitably, coffins fall and visitors then arrange the bones within the caves.
A cave might be dedicated solely to a particular family, but more commonly
it serves an entire village. Some sites—such as the burial grounds near Bua
(above; pp.66—67), Londa (p.70), and Lombok (pp.71, 73)—combine
bones with striking geological formations to create stunning displays. The
only exceptions to this burial tradition are made for babies; they are placed
within holes in tarra trees, which have a white sap, symbolizing mother's milk.

71

The largest displays of bones are found
behind the village of Ke'te Kesu. This
small mountain township is home to
what is believed to be the oldest of the
extant burial grounds, Bukit Buntu Kesu
(below; pp.74–75). The site has served
the deceased for over 700 years—longer
than the current village has even been in
existence. Bukit Buntu Kesu is also unique
in that the bones are not displayed inside
the local cave, but instead arranged outside
the entrance. Rather than a burial cave, the
site is in fact a large charnel ground, and as
one climbs a steep and winding path behind
the village towards the cave mouth, groups
of bones are encountered at intervals
along the way, having fallen from coffins
suspended on the face of the mountain wall.

Torajan coffins such as these are known as *erong*,
and while they are expensive to produce and show
skilled workmanship, like the deceased they also
undergo a process of decay. It is notable that many
coffins feature carved buffalo heads (p.78). Tombs
cut into burial rocks, where many wealthy Torajans
are now buried, might likewise include doors
showing buffalo in relief or have actual horns
attached to them (p.79). Buffalo are an important
component of the funeral ceremony and are
slaughtered in memory of the deceased, often
in large numbers because the more important
the person, the greater the sacrifice that must be
made. These animals have important symbolic
significance to the post-mortem journey, since it
is believed that buffalo are necessary in order to
travel onward to the land of souls.

Similar burial caves are found on the island of Luzon in the Philippines, where tribal members likewise used them as cemetery grounds. Large numbers of green weathered coffins are found in the Lumiang Cave near the town of Sagada (above). Stacked on the floor and wedged into ledges around the cave's ominous maw, they were placed here in order to symbolically return the deceased to their earthen mother. Also found in Sagada is a cliff with coffins wedged into fissures of the rock, giving the impression that they are dangling in mid-air. The displays near Sagada are deceptive, because many more coffins are in fact present, with older burials being wedged further back into crevices. Bones are not seen at these sites, but are prominent at other caves in the region.

The Opdas Cave (above; pp.82–83), located west of Sagada in the town of Kabayan, is the most extensive display of human remains in the Philippines. Containing several hundred skulls between 500 and 1,000 years old, Opdas was unearthed by local resident Baban Berong in 1971. Berong believed he heard the voices of many people speaking to him from beneath the rear of his property and, upon digging, discovered a burial cave. It was not possible to determine how the remains were originally arranged, but Berong spent years clearing out the cave and adding the ledges on which skulls are now presented. His descendants continue to live on the property and report that the dead still speak to them, affirming the special connection they have with those who passed on centuries ago.

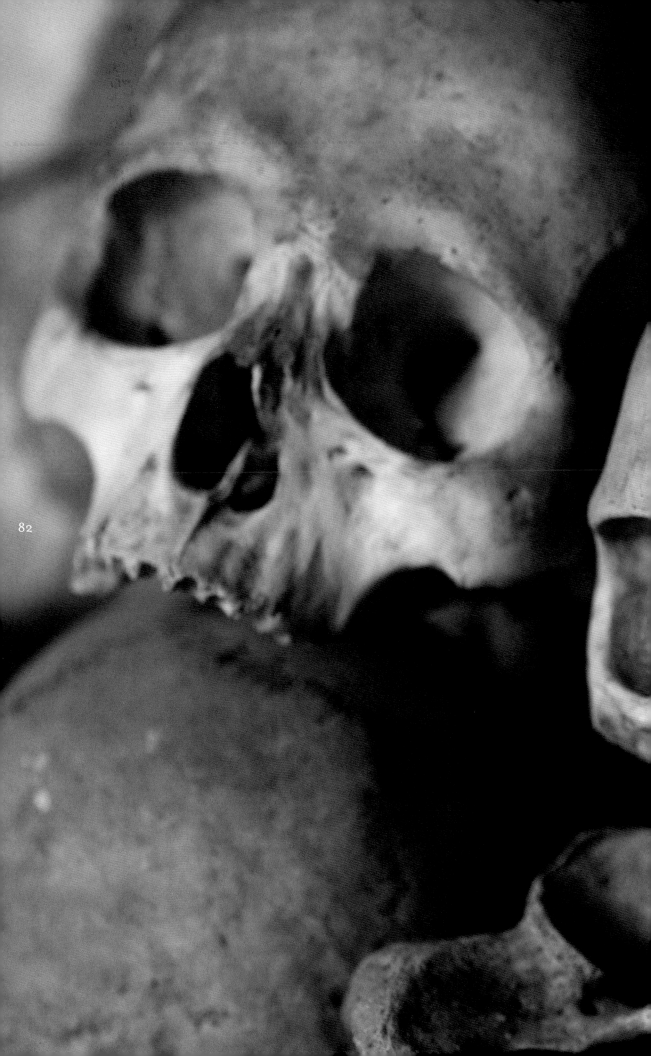

82

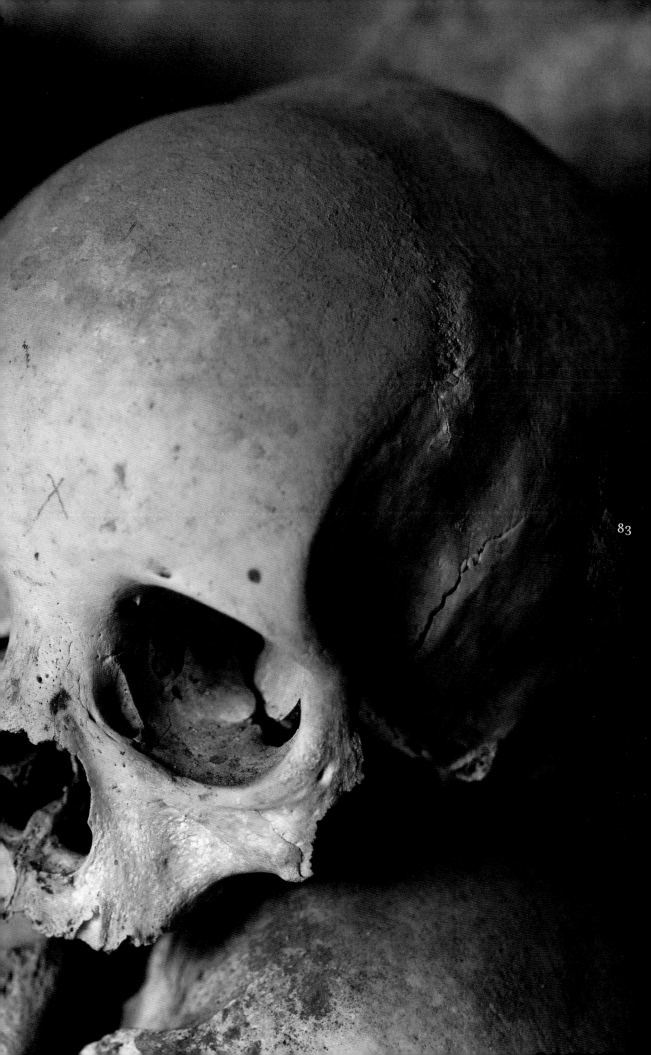

Blessed Souls

💀　💀　💀

In the Catholic world, a golden age of art in human bone dawned in the late sixteenth century. To refute Protestant claims that the Church was rife with luxury and worldliness, its visual culture began to express extreme morbidity. Especially in monasteries, death was embraced in tangible form, and simple charnel houses were often rearranged into complex statements of "memento mori." Eventually, parish churches and even confraternities dedicated to death were creating extravagant displays in bone. Some of these ossuaries possessed staggering beauty, such as San Bernardino alle Ossa in Milan (opposite), where the bones had acquired a cult following by the mid-seventeenth century, and the chapel's continued popularity caused it to be reconstructed in the 1750s into its current, glorious form.

85

Other charnels were built to massive scale, such as a twenty-meter-long bone chapel in Evora, Portugal (pp.86–87). Constructed by Franciscan monks in the early seventeenth century, it was known locally as the "House of Disillusion." and intended to inspire repentance. A pair of mummies was even included, one a man, the other a child, hung high on the right-hand wall. The trend for elaborate ossuaries also migrated to Eastern Europe. Among the most impressive examples is the Kaplica Czaszek (Chapel of Skulls) in Czermna, Poland (below; opposite). Founded in 1776 by the priest Waclaw Tomaszek, it provided a space for special services on All Souls' Day. Legend holds that the skulls of Tomaszek and his gravedigger, who did most of the construction, were added to the display after they died.

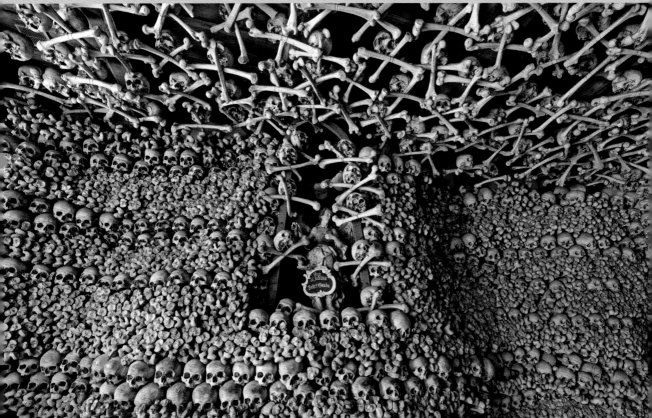

Extravagant charnels became especially popular in the Czech Republic during the eighteenth century. A tetrahedral-shaped ossuary was constructed next to the Church of St Bartolomějeme in Kolín in 1733 with bones exhumed from the churchyard cemetery, and then rebuilt in its current appearance in 1850 (p.90). Its high walls support a life-sized Crucifixion, and towering bone obelisks dwarf the visitor. As a final touch, a fully articulated skeleton holding a scythe was added in 1851. Another outstanding charnel was constructed in the village of Nížkov (p.91; below). The remains of some 8,000 people, most of them soldiers killed in local battles, were arranged into four large stacks in a neoclassical style, and annual services to commemorate the dead were held in the room.

Charnels could also function to memorialize victims of tragedy. For example, in 1766, the remains of nearly a thousand people who had been killed by a fire thirty-four years previously in the Portuguese town of Campo Maior were used to construct an ossuary chapel dedicated in their memory. The design included three complete, articulated skeletons set into the walls (opposite). Bone houses as memorials became especially popular in Italy in the nineteenth century, serving as tributes to those who had died in battles in the northern part of the country. Major ossuaries were constructed to war dead in churches in Solferino, San Martino (pp.94–95), and Custoza, and were meant to honor the cause of peace by demonstrating that enemies on the battlefield were now brothers-in-arms in death.

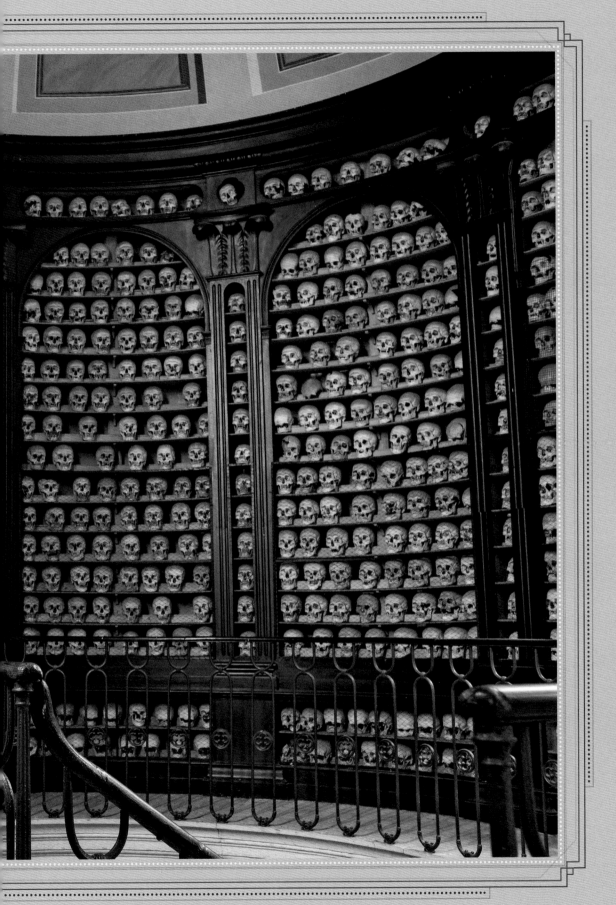

Considered liminal spaces where the living and dead could interact, charnels often acquired cult followings. A cave system in Naples known as the Fontanelle Cemetery was a dumping ground for human remains, and became a popular site of devotion. Prayers were offered to the skulls in the hope that the dead would in turn use their powers to assist the living. Favored skulls might even be enshrined by those who adored them (opposite). Such practices seem disconnected from modern Catholicism, but similar veneration is found in remote areas such as Lampa, Peru. An extensive ossuary was created there as a burial site for a local aristocrat (pp.98–99); offerings are still left in front of skulls placed on the tomb's windows in an attempt to commune with the dead (above).

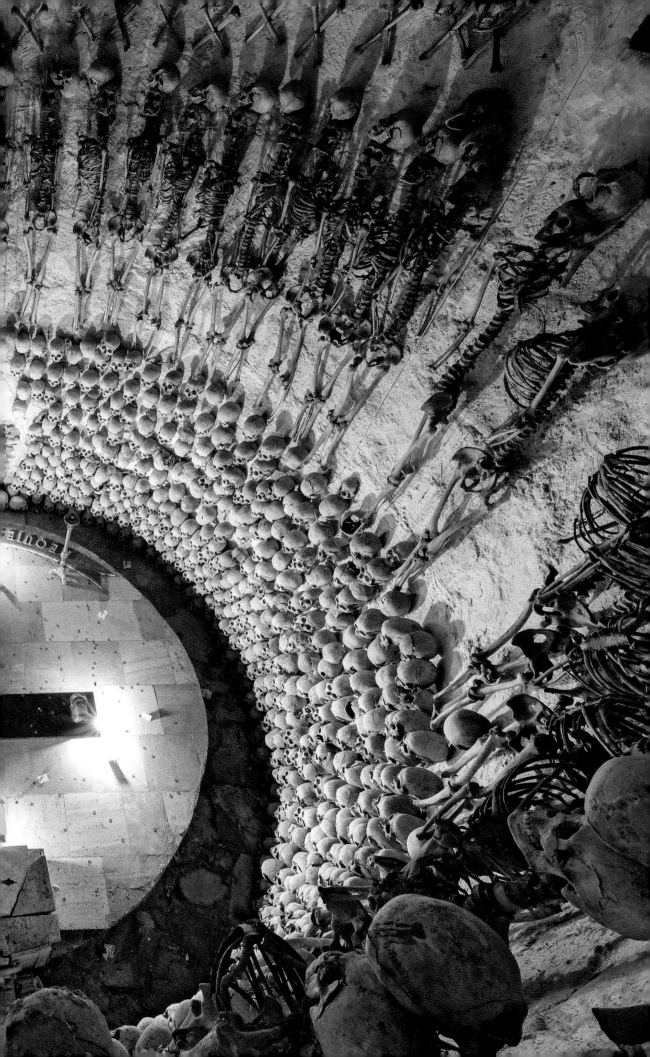

Many of the great Catholic bone rooms did not survive. Having lost their significance as the relationship with the dead changed in Western culture, they fell into disrepair and were destroyed, known now only as historical footnotes. Yet a few were recovered by the modern world and rebuilt as testimony to their historical value. These include a medieval ossuary in Brno, Czech Republic (opposite). Sealed off and buried under the Church of St James, it now stands complete after a decade-long restoration. A similar effort revived a charnel in Eggenburg, Austria (below). But the most dramatic example is in Mělník, Czech Republic, where skulls placed within a lengthy wall of bones spell out the words *Ecce Mors*, or "Behold Death"—death was again placed on display here, after an extensive reconstruction returned a forgotten ossuary to glory (pp.102–103).

They Shall Not Perish

MEMORIALS IN BONE TO VICTIMS OF TRAGEDY

💀 💀 💀

As spiritual sites, ossuaries may now seem archaic, but that does not mean they are no longer constructed: they have been adopted as poignant memorials to those who perished in modern tragedies. The largest such monument is on the outskirts of Phnom Penh, Cambodia. Built in 1988 and standing a staggering 62 meters high, it is a Buddhist stupa on the site of a former orchard at Choeung Ek (opposite), commemorating casualties of the Khmer Rouge's reign of terror. Up to 1.5 million people were killed during the Cambodian genocide of 1975-1979, and 5,000 skulls discovered in the orchard are housed behind the tower's glass walls. The display includes placards indicating victims who were singled out because of their ethnicity (pp.106-107), providing a powerful reminder to the global community of the consequences of intolerance and the violence that was committed here.

ស្ត្រីកាស់ជ័ពជនជាតិកម្ពុជ[...]

SENILE FEMALE KAMP[...]

រនអាយុលើសពី 60ឆ្នាំឡើង

AN OVER 60 YEARS OLD

The greatest number of genocide memorials are found throughout Rwanda, tributes to the estimated million people killed there in 1994, when ethnic Hutus with elite positions in the government and army unleashed a killing spree against the Tutsi minority. Despite pleas for intervention, Western powers stood by inactive, leaving the Rwandans to settle their own bloody affairs. Many Tutsis turned to the Catholic Church for protection, but were either rebuffed or betrayed, and it is in churches that some of the most poignant memorials have been constructed, with the clothing of those massacred piled high over pews in a silent expression of loss and grief. The tragic episode lasted for only a hundred days, but its wake left twenty percent of the country dead, including seventy percent of ethnic Tutsis.

Recounting a litany of terror, genocide memorials are found throughout
Rwanda. A large display is found at Bisesero, where 30,000 Tutsis were killed;
the site is known as the "Hill of Resistance," due to the valiant but ultimately futile
attempts of the populace to fight off their attackers. A tribute is also found at a
convent in Nyarubuye, where 20,000 people attempting to escape to Tanzania
were massacred. Another memorial, composed of bones and mummified
remains, is found at Murambi Technical School, where 45,000 perished—large
groups of Tutsis had tried to hide in a local church, but were betrayed by the
mayor and bishop. Lured to the school as a supposed safe haven, they were left to
defend themselves with stones, and eventually overrun and slaughtered.

114

Rwanda's capital city of Kigali also contains a memorial center (p.111 top right), and larger tributes are found nearby at Nyamata and Ntarama. The former was the site of the massacre of some 45,000 Tutsis, including 10,000 who perished inside the church where the memorial is housed (p.108; p.109; p.110). Rural Ntarama, meanwhile, saw some of the most brutal killings of the genocide. Over 5,000 people fled to the local red brick chapel hoping to find refuge, but they instead found death; their bones pummeled and broken by assassins, and their skulls cleaved with machetes. The victims and all their possessions remain at Ntarama to this day: their remains are set into racks, and their clothing hangs from the rafters, creating a painful display condemning the senseless violence that nearly destroyed an entire country (p.111 top left and bottom; pp.112–113; p.114; below).

Remains to be Seen

MUMMIES AND OTHER EXQUISITE CORPSES

💀　💀　💀

In addition to bones, sometimes entire bodies are placed on display in memorial. This was especially popular in parts of Catholic Europe from the late sixteenth to early nineteenth centuries. It was particularly common in Italy for confraternities of death, the charitable brotherhoods that provided burials for the poor and indigent, to mummify members of their group and put them on view as statements of prestige and morbid piety. The most impressive surviving collection is in Oria (opposite; pp.118-119). Brothers of the local confraternity who left a testament indicating a desire to be mummified would be prepared by having their brains removed, their intestines replaced with fragrant herbs, and their bodies submerged in chalk for two years. Afterwards, they would be fully dehydrated and cleaned, then placed in a niche under the town's cathedral.

118

The Catholic trend for displaying mummies started in Capuchin monasteries. When the order began construction on a new property in Rome in 1631, the brothers brought with them 300 cartloads of bones with which to construct what was at the time Europe's most extravagant charnel, spread out over a six-room crypt. However, the monks had more than a charnel in mind. As members of their community died, they were mummified by their own brethren and added to the display (pp.120–121; p.122; p.123; below), and when there was no more room for mummies, they were buried under the floor. Christened Santa Maria della Concezione, the site set a new benchmark in macabre decor due to its combination of mummies, grave markers, and sophisticated designs in bone.

It was in Sicily that the real vanguard of Catholic mummification was found (pp.128–129), particularly in Palermo, where Capuchin monks began preparing bodies in 1599 beneath the monastery of Santa Maria della Pace. The deceased were naturally dehydrated, pickled in a vinegar solution, and then displayed in niches. Initially, the monks used the process only on Capuchin brothers, but the monastery's crypt became so renowned that lay people began to request mummification for their loved ones. The preparation of bodies became a cottage industry for the monks, and several galleries were constructed for the display of cadavers. Dubbed the Palermo Catacombs, the site housed 3,000 mummies (pp.125–127; opposite). From Palermo, the trend for mummification would spread with the Capuchins to smaller towns nearby, such as Burgio (below; p.132; p.133).

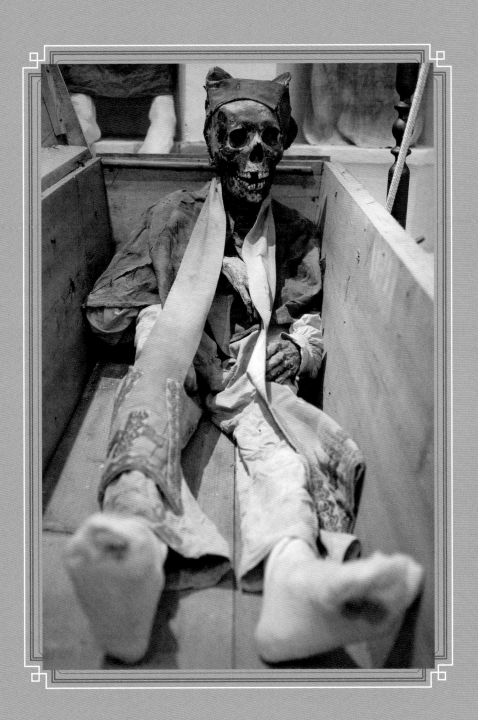

Capuchin convents eventually created mummies throughout Sicily. Bodies prepared by the monks are still found from Comiso on the south coast to Savoca in the north-east, as well as in remote villages such as Pettineo (opposite). Mummification was not confined to the Capuchins, however, and eventually gained popularity in a variety of local churches. While many of the collections in parish churches have been destroyed, small numbers of mummies still survive in towns such as Caccamo (below), where the bodies preserved were eighteenth-century members of a confraternity dedicated to souls in Purgatory. In Gangi, nearly a hundred mummies of priests who had served at the Church of St Nicholas of Bari are still found in the church's crypt (pp.134–135). Aside from Palermo, most of these other collections are scarcely known to outsiders.

Families were expected to tend to their dead relatives. Unless special arrangements had been made between the deceased and the church that administered the crypt, the living needed to pay rent on the niche in which the mummy was placed, lest it be removed from view. Visits would also be paid to the dead, in particular on November 2, the Catholic All Souls' Day. This was an occasion for the family to assemble in the crypt, offer prayers for the mummy, and dress it in new clothes for the coming year. The deceased would also be scented with perfume and female corpses might be given a bouquet to hold. The result was an intimate bond with the dead that is almost unmatched in the annals of history.

Displays of mummies soon became popular across Catholic Europe, as the trend traveled with the monastic orders. The identities of the mummified man and child in Evora, Portugal (opposite), are unknown, but placed in the context of the prodigious display of mortality surrounding them, they help create a statement about the Ages of Man from infancy to death. Mummies proved especially popular in the Czech Republic, where two large collections were established. One was created by Jesuits in Klatovy in the seventeenth and eighteenth centuries (below). Originally there were around 200 mummies, but only thirty-five have survived. The other group was in Brno, the product of Capuchins who desired a crypt along the lines of their brothers in Palermo and Rome when they founded their monastery in 1651.

Europe is not the only place where mummies were important to the living. Near the village of Kabayan in north Luzon, Philippines, Ibaloi tribesmen traditionally preserved their dead through a lengthy process that included desiccating the body over a fire and blowing tobacco smoke into the mouth of the deceased. Hundreds of burial caves dotted the surrounding mountainous terrain. The spirits of those who had passed on were believed to have the power to preserve balance in the world, and the mummies were appealed to during times of hardship. Disapproving Spanish colonial overlords put an end to the practice, so most of the surviving mummies date to before the sixteenth century. Nevertheless, veneration of the bodies has continued, and burial caves are still visited, their locations kept secret by tribal leaders (below; opposite).

Venerated in Asia,
mummified Buddhist
monks are known by various
terms, including full-body
śarīras (relics) and flesh-
body *bodhisattvas*, and their
incorruptible state is seen
as a sign of holiness. The
mummies are created by
natural processes, with
the most famous school
of mummification known
as *Sokushinbutsu*. Popular in
Japan during the eleventh
century, it was a form of
preservation begun while the
practitioner was still alive
and involved 1,000 days of
dieting, followed by 1,000
days of drinking a poisonous
tea, then 1,000 days spent in
a locked tomb. The practice
was outlawed and few of
the *Sokushinbutsu* mummies are
preserved, but monks whose
bodies remain incorrupt are
still treated as sacred in the
Buddhist world — some are
even gilded and regarded as
living statuary (opposite).

It is not known when bodies were first gilded, but the practice is now associated with esoteric and localized forms of veneration. Normally such treatment was reserved for monks but, in some cases, even important women might be gilded. Two recent examples are found in Taiwan. The golden corpse of Dexiu (opposite) is enshrined in a temple in Jilong, where Daoist and Buddhist practices are fused. Dexiu was a famed spirit medium, known to channel indigenous Taiwanese gods. She prophesied her own death in 1993, and gave instructions for her preservation so that she could continue to serve the local community. Gongga (above) was a nun from the Kagyu school, a Tibetan order of Buddhism, who was preserved and gilded when she died in Taipei in 1997.

Gilded bodies comprise only a minority of Buddhist mummies – most are simply preserved as naked flesh and placed in temples as examples of exceptional faith. Luang Por Daeng (below) is preserved at Khun Arum temple on the Thai island of Koh Samui. He asked before his death in 1973 that if his body did not decay, it be put on display. His wish was granted and he has become immensely popular with tourists, due in no small part to his fashionable sunglasses. Daeng is not the only mummy on Koh Samui, however. The body of Luang Por Ruam (opposite) is enshrined at Wat Kiri Wongkaram, where he was a member of the monastic community until his death in 1966. His fingernails continue to grow to this day, and clippings are taken as charms.

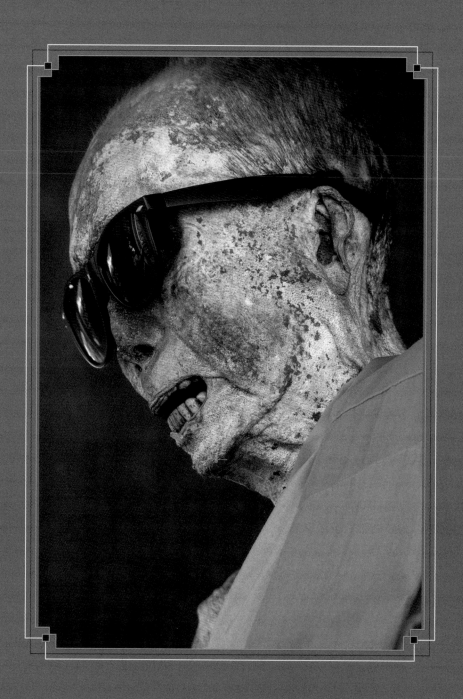

The tradition of intentional mummification in South America is as old as
any in the world. In some cultures, mummies of important people were
meant to be seen and venerated; the Inca, for instance, placed their dead
king on a throne, covered his body in silver and gold pieces, and exposed him
during special ceremonies. Such mummies were destroyed by the Spanish,
but numerous others survive, sometimes in situ. Several are preserved at the
Chauchilla necropolis in Peru, where the Nazca buried their dead between
AD 200 and 900 (opposite; above; below). Placed in seated postures,
they face east, towards the rising sun. Heads buried alongside them were
apparently those of community members. Many other mummies are also
found in their tombs at sites in Chile and Bolivia (pp.152–153).

151

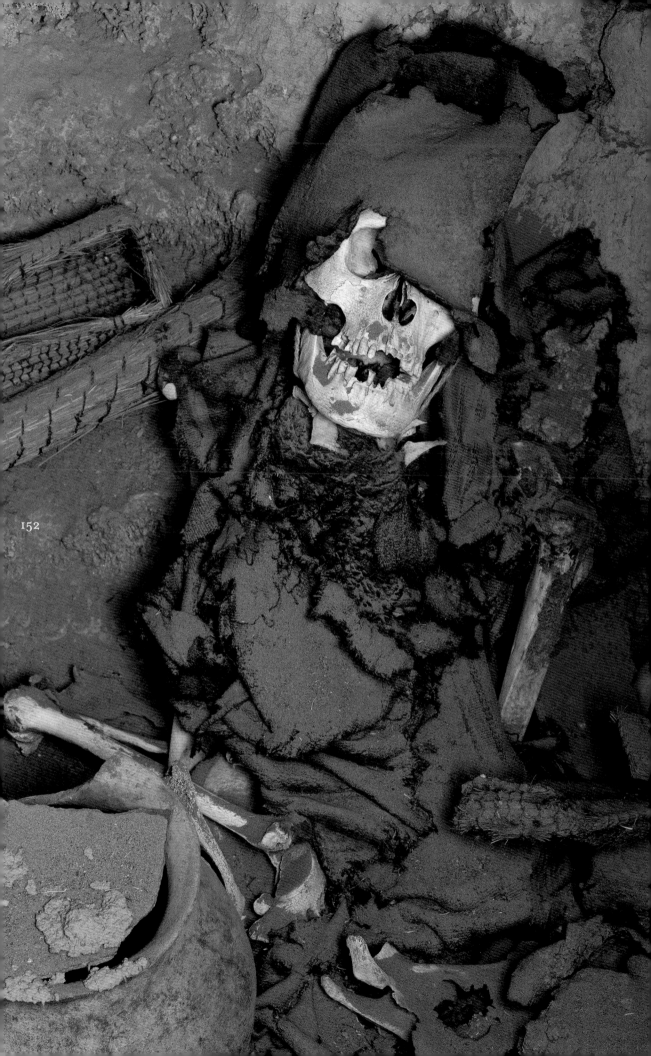

152

Crossing the Border

The most emphatic modern example of the connection with the dead is found in Bolivia. As part of a continuing cultural tradition, many people own skulls known as "ñatitas" (a nickname roughly meaning "the little pug-nosed ones"), which are enshrined within the home and considered esteemed friends or family members (opposite; pp.156-157). "Ñatitas" may provide any number of services, as guardians of the domicile, trusted advisors, spiritual guides, or simply good-luck charms. The roots of the practice can be traced to long-standing indigenous beliefs concerning the interaction between the living and the dead. For the Aymara Indians of the Bolivian highlands, death was never a fatalistic concept. Those who passed on had simply transcended to another phase of life, and could still function within the family or social group.

155

Most commonly associated with La Paz, El Alto, and the surrounding countryside, the practice of keeping *ñatitas* crosses social strata to include people from all walks of life. A person would typically possess only a single skull but some people own a considerable number — one home counts fifty-four, all kept in individual shrines. Often these people are *yatiri*, an Aymara term for healers who have a role analogous to a shaman. In such cases, their residence might be considered equivalent to a temple, with the individual *ñatitas* believed to exercise different powers. Skulls may specialize in anything from domestic problems to schoolwork or medical issues, and residents of the neighborhood can visit such a home in order to seek appropriate assistance.

NO TOCAR NI
RAYAR LAS
URNAS DE LAS
ÑATITAS

RAMIRO

PEDRO

Pedro

PEDRO
✝
Q.E.P.D.

NO LLOREN NO HE MUERTO MORIRE
CUNADO USTEDES SE HAYAN OLVIDADO

Skulls that serve as *ñatitas* may have been obtained from medical schools, found at archeological sites, or acquired when the deceased are removed from cemeteries due to non-payment of fees — small white eviction notices are a common sight in La Paz's Cemetery General (above; opposite). This means that despite the expectations of outsiders, the skulls are typically not those of relatives or close friends. A lack of familiarity with the deceased is not an obstacle, since the identity of the soul that communicates through the skull is not necessarily that of the formerly living person. In Aymara belief, spiritual nature is complex and the soul is not a discrete entity, but rather composed of several distinct facets. When a skull is taken as a *ñatita*, the spirit centralized around it will reveal an identity directly to its owner, often in dreams.

The veneration of the skulls is pervasive enough that adherents are even found on the police force. There is a pair of *ñatitas* enshrined in the homicide division of the national law enforcement agency FELCC (Fuerza Especial de Lucha Contra el Crimen, or "The Special Force to Battle Crime") in El Alto. Named Juanito and Juanita, the latter has been with the unit for three decades, while the former's tenure is so long that no one is sure when he arrived — some claim he may have been with the local police for a century, and he has affectionately been called the longest-serving officer on the force. By providing assistance to detectives in the form of clues to difficult cases, the skulls have been credited with helping to solve hundreds of crimes.

Juanito and Juanita are similarly dressed in knitted caps and wideband
sunglasses (above; opposite). Traditional veneration involves officers saying
prayers in their honor and writing requests for information on slips of paper
that are placed in their shrines. In return for their services, the pair is provided
with gifts and offerings, which commonly include coca leaves, cigarettes, votive
candles, and candy. The skulls have also been used in interrogation, since it is
believed that it would be impossible to lie in their presence. Not surprisingly,
detractors claim that their effect is psychological rather than metaphysical.
But as a former division commander explained, whatever the source of their
power, the skulls bring tangible benefits: he estimated that using the *ñatitas* cut
investigation time in half on difficult cases.

Normally a hidden force, *ñatitas* become a spectacular public presence on November 8, the date of their holiday, the annual *Fiesta de las Ñatitas* (opposite; below; pp.164–185). The skulls are removed from their homes and taken to local cemeteries for a celebration in their honor—in particular, the Cemetery General in La Paz, where thousands of people congregate. Shortly after daybreak, the *ñatitas* begin to arrive, cradled tenderly in makeshift shrines or cardboard boxes. Carefully dressed for the occasion, many sport dark glasses to protect them from the sun's glare and hats to ward off the cold morning air. Taken first into the cemetery chapel to hear a Mass, the skulls are then placed in hastily constructed altars outside the chapel, where offerings are made in thanks for a year of devoted service.

163

Serenaded by wandering musicians and surrounded by well-wishers, the skulls in the cemetery are proudly displayed throughout the grounds. To give the *ñatitas* sight, cotton balls are pressed into their empty eye sockets, and lips might also be created by molding wax or metal foil over their bony jaws. Common tributes given to them include coca leaves, candles, and incense, but they are also frequently offered cigarettes, candy, pastries and breads, and cups of alcohol or soda. It is flowers, however, that are the most ubiquitous motif at the *Fiesta*. Petals are copiously strewn among the skulls, which are also crowned with floral wreaths. The souls rejoice in beautiful things, and the panoply of brilliant colors provided by the flowers is the best offering of all.

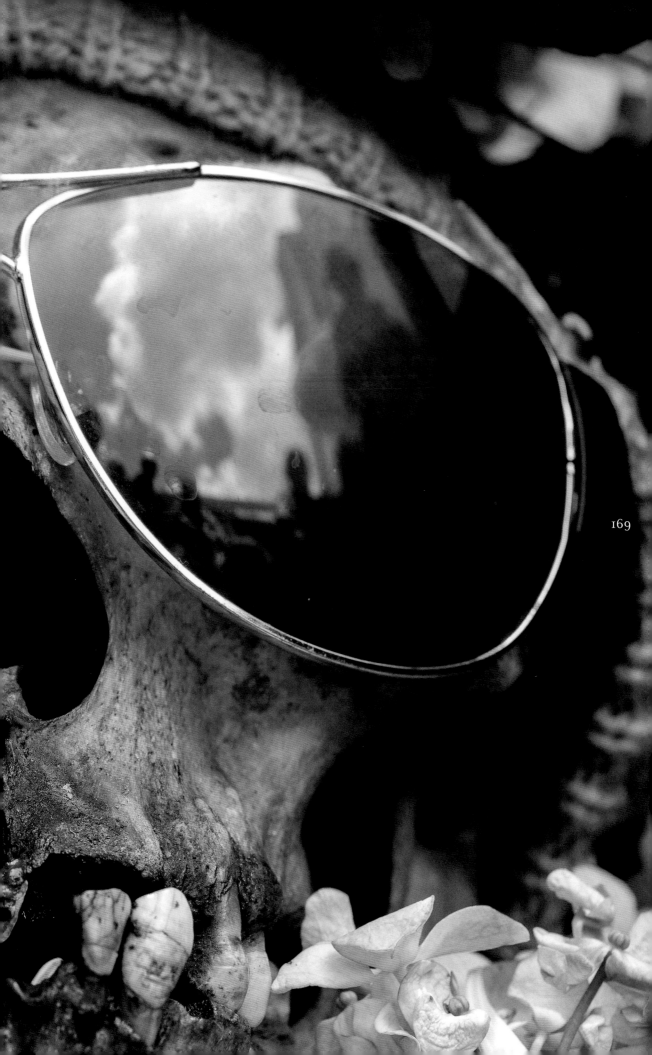

The context in which *ñatitas* are presented can vary radically, with some placed humbly upon a simple cloth, others carried in sedan chairs like royalty, or set into elaborate displays. Meanwhile, some of the skulls appear in emulation of those who care for them, or in a way that indicates their profession. Military officers, for instance, might present their *ñatitas* wearing their uniform hats or surrounded by their service medals, and dentists often provide their skulls with prosthetic teeth, meticulously set to ensure the jaws reveal a perfect smile. Despite these differences, one thing that everyone gathered at the cemetery is agreed upon is that the *Fiesta de las Ñatitas* is in no way a celebration of death—rather, it is a celebration of a bond, one that is intimate and unique.

More than simply a time to thank the *ñatitas* for their past services, the *Fiesta* is also an opportunity to reaffirm the bond between skull and owner, and ensure a continued relationship. Various forms of divination are believed to be possible with the *ñatitas*, and some celebrants use the occasion to prognosticate fortunes for the upcoming year. Cigarette ashes can provide potential portents, with white being positive and black negative. Coca leaves can also be used to augur: first placed in the mouth of a skull, they are then chewed by a medium who makes predictions based on their sweetness. Even the patterns of melted wax that drip from the votive candles offered to a *ñatita* can be read to reveal future events.

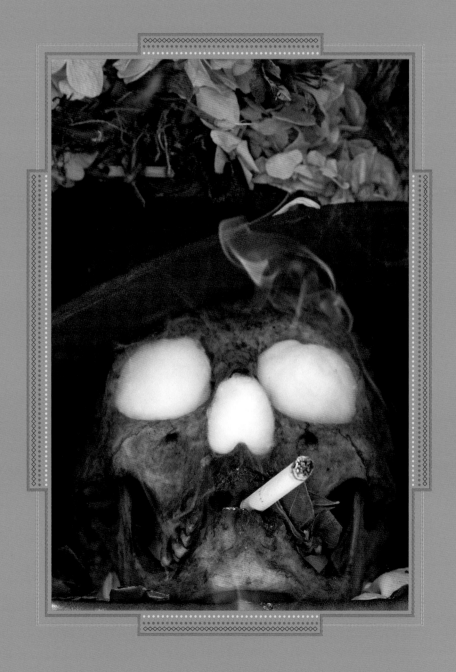

The use of skulls for religious or magical purposes dates back to Pre-Columbian times in the Bolivian highlands, where crania were, among other things, believed to have curative powers and aid in weather control and agricultural fertility. Catholicism was imposed by the Spanish but, rather than being eradicated, local ideas about the role of the dead in society instead adapted and evolved. The Church officially disavows any connection to the skulls, but in fact the foundation of the contemporary *Fiesta* is a complex syncretism between the Catholic cult of the dead and indigenous beliefs. While the Western world may have turned its back on such practices long ago, the veneration offered to the *ñatitas* testifies to the vital connection that is possible between the living and the dead.

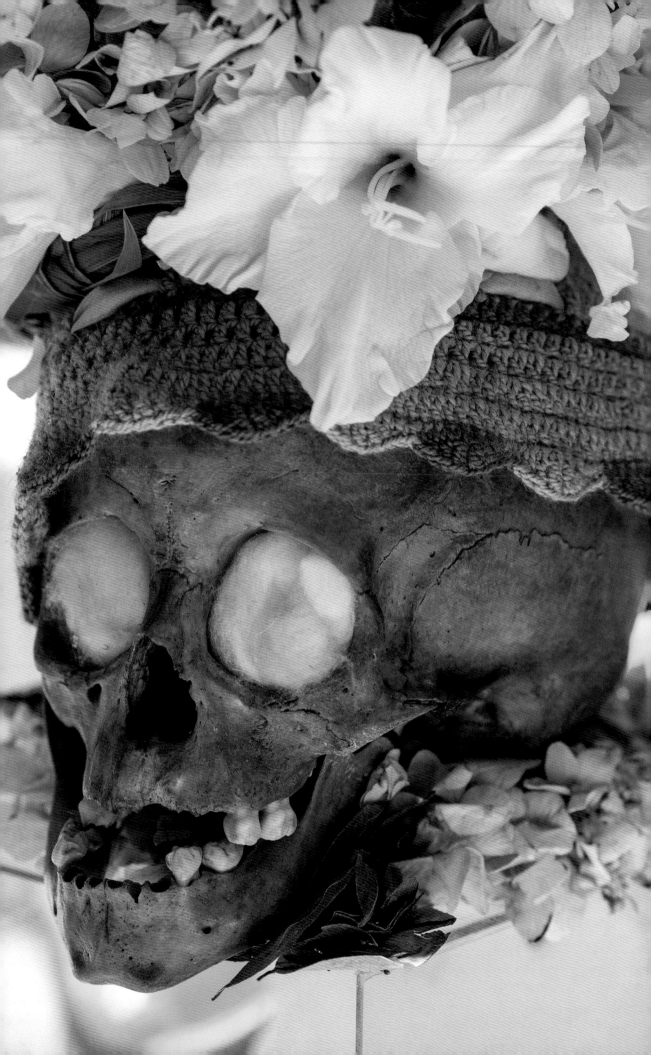

Johann Pfandl
1880

aa Pfandl
vulgo Stillin.

na Pfa

Heavenly Glory

The often flamboyant treatment of
the "ñatitas" in Bolivia is only one
manifestation of a historically popular
practice. Decorating bones has been
a common feature in diverse cultures,
providing a means to respect and even
venerate the dead by creating icons
from their remains. One of the most
enduring forms of decoration was
the painting of skulls in small villages
in Bavaria, Austria, and Switzerland;
a practice that began in the early
eighteenth century, and lasted in some
areas into the twentieth. Having one's
skull painted was a sign of status, and
considered an honor bestowed upon
the deceased by loving relatives. Since
the name was included on the skull, it
also helped preserve kinship bonds by
preventing the deceased from falling
into anonymity within the bone pile.

187

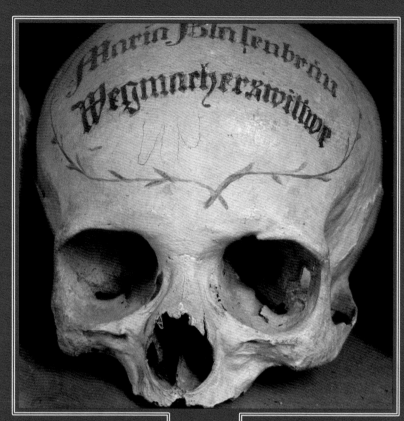

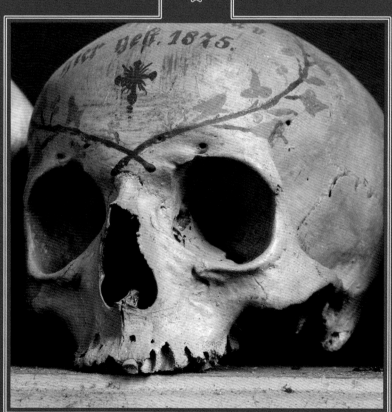

Painted either by local gravediggers or traveling artists, the decorated crania were integrated into family life when adults brought children into the charnel houses and related stories about the people whose skulls were on display. As the bone rooms fell out of use, the painted skulls were typically buried in common graves in local cemeteries. Many of those not interred vanished through other means, sometimes stolen as mementos or taken to museums, and few large collections remain intact. The most appreciable is in Hallstatt, Austria, where the town's ossuary still displays over 600 painted skulls (p.186; p.188; below). Dingolfing, Germany (opposite), also preserves a sizeable collection in its old bone house, and isolated examples can be found in various surviving ossuaries in small towns throughout the Alps (p.189).

One of the more curious contemporary uses for decorated skulls is found in Bangkok, Thailand. A group of a dozen crania covered in flaking gold leaf, with small gold lamé cushions inserted in their eye sockets, sit in a red lacquer shrine at the office of a foundation that provides free coffins for poor families and the indigent dead (opposite; pp.194–195). The skulls are considered patrons of dead paupers and John Does, and their spirits each cover different parts of the city to watch over the newly deceased, helping to ensure that no harm comes to the body before it is placed in a coffin, or otherwise disposed of with dignity. Equally important, they prevent the spirits of the dead from lingering and becoming ghosts by comforting them in their time of transition.

Known as *Ruamkatanyu*, the foundation was established by a merchant named Somikiat who, out of the goodness of his heart, began paying for funerals for poor people. It also operates a longstanding volunteer ambulance company, and it is said that the skulls were those of early ambulance patients from the 1950s who died while being transported to a hospital. After their bodies went unclaimed, a shrine was constructed in the organization's warehouse to house their skulls and give them a respectful home. Now the souls of the original twelve deceased have a chance to aid others by assisting restless spirits—in essence, representing yet another charitable arm of the foundation. Their work is rewarded by offerings made in their honor and a special annual holiday during which they are re-gilded.

Ornate skulls known as *kapala* were traditionally produced in monasteries in Tibet, Nepal, and Northern India, where they were used as ritual vessels in both Hindu and Buddhist Tantra (opposite; pp.198–199). Topped by a hinged or removable cap, the skull itself is typically lined with a silver bowl, into which wine or dough cakes are placed. The *kapala* aid the user in attaining a transcendental state by transferring the knowledge and personality of the deceased. They also provide a reminder of the impermanence of life and the importance of avoiding sensual indulgence. Traditionally collected at sky burial sites—where the bodies of the dead were dismembered and scattered over open ground—the skulls were elaborately carved or decorated with precious metals and jewels, then anointed and consecrated.

The most lavishly decorated
bones are those of full
skeletons from the Roman
Catacombs, identified as
Early Christian martyrs in the
sixteenth through eighteenth
centuries, and transported
primarily to Germany,
Austria and Switzerland.
The skeletons were decorated
by nuns who were skilled in
textile and beadwork, or lay
brothers who had trained as
gold- and silversmiths. The
bones would be articulated
and covered over with jewels
(pp.204–215), or placed in
finely wrought suits of armor
with cutouts strategically
placed to reveal their skeletal
nature (pp.200–201).
Products of the Catholic
battle against Protestantism,
these macabre masterpieces
were intended to help
reinvigorate faith locally by
providing an unmistakable
reminder of the honors that
were reserved for those who
made the greatest sacrifices
for the Church.

Real jewels were frequently used to line the opulent bones, but even when they were imitations they would have been outlandishly expensive, since only a handful of glassmakers in Europe could create presentation-quality artificial gems. Often the skeletons were robed in clothing provided by local aristocrats that had been specially tailored to to accentuate their bony physiques. A custom wardrobe might even be devised, sometimes to create the image of *Miles Christi*, or "soldier of Christ," by elaborately imitating the style of ancient Roman armor (p.207). The extravagance was such that many of the skeletons were given wigs made of gold or silver wire. The work could take years to complete but the final effect was one of total transformation, as raw bones become tangible examples of Heavenly Glory

Although none of these skeletons was ever officially canonized, they were enshrined
in altars and venerated as saints. Miracles were often attributed to them and the most
popular became inseparable parts of local identity for the towns in which they were
displayed. Many were surrounded by ex-votos, as thanks for the supernatural assistance
they were believed to have provided. The shrines of those considered to have exceptional
powers, such as St Felix in Gars-am-Inn, Germany (p. 209), became popular pilgrimage
sites, drawing not only locals but also foreigners who had heard about the skeletons'
fame. Others acquired cult followings as patrons of underprivileged classes:
St Munditia in Munich (pp. 204–205), for example, became a favorite of spinsters,
and older, unmarried women flocked to her as their protectress.

The process used to authenticate the bones had been slipshod, relying on often faulty circumstantial evidence. In truth, few of the decorated skeletons could be proven to have been martyrs, and during the Enlightenment their popularity waned. By the late eighteenth century, some churches had already removed them due to a lack of firm provenance, and in the early nineteenth century many were destroyed when a wave of church secularization left large numbers of the "catacomb saints" homeless. Considered as questionable ecclesiastic items to be liquidated from decommissioned churches, the skeletons' precious adornments were frequently stripped away and their bones discarded as rubbish. Those that survive, however, are testaments to a different age, one in which death was not an impassable boundary, allowing the dead a vital role to play among the living.

PAUL KOUDOUNARIS is an author and photographer who specializes in the visual culture of death. Studying the use of human bones as a form of remembrance, he has traveled the world to document their presence in sacred environments. His book *The Empire of Death* (2011) was the first ever in-depth history of ossuaries, and *Heavenly Bodies* (2013) was a study of lavishly decorated Baroque skeletons taken from the Roman Catacombs. Both have been widely acclaimed not only as photographic works, but also for their contributions to history, anthropology, and religious studies.
He lives in Los Angeles and has a PhD in Art History from UCLA.

The author wishes to express his thanks and admiration for all of those people who work devotedly to maintain the sites depicted in this book. Without your efforts, this poignant past would be lost, and the dead would truly perish.

FIRST PUBLISHED IN THE UNITED KINGDOM IN 2015 BY
THAMES & HUDSON LTD, 181A HIGH HOLBORN, LONDON WC1V 7QX

FIRST PUBLISHED IN THE UNITED STATES OF AMERICA IN 2015 BY
THAMES & HUDSON INC., 500 FIFTH AVENUE, NEW YORK, NEW YORK 10110

THIS COMPACT EDITION FIRST PUBLISHED IN 2022
REPRINTED 2023

Memento Mori: The Dead Among Us © 2015 Dr Paul Koudounaris

Design: Barnbrook

British Library Cataloguing-in-Publication Data
A catalogue record for this book is available from the British Library

Library of Congress Control Number 2014944638

ISBN 978-0-500-25261-1

Printed and bound in Slovenia by DZS-Grafik d.o.o.

Be the first to know about our new releases, exclusive content and author events by visiting
thamesandhudson.com
thamesandhudsonusa.com
thamesandhudson.com.au

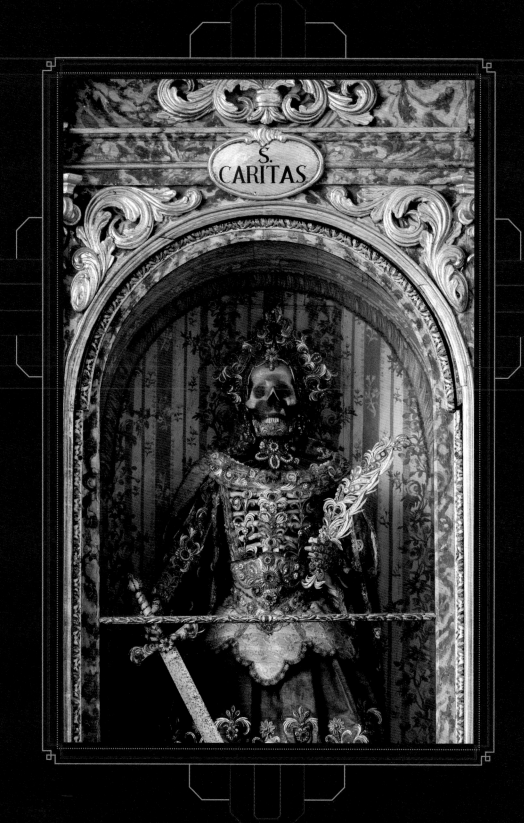